CW01513003

Original title:

Indigo Shifts Above the Phoenix Carp

Copyright © 2025 Swan Charm

All rights reserved.

Author: Aron Pilviste

ISBN HARDBACK: 978-1-80563-225-2

ISBN PAPERBACK: 978-1-80564-746-1

Veils of Twilight

In the hush of evening light,
Whispers echo, dreams take flight.
Shadows weave through ancient trees,
A serenade upon the breeze.

Stars awaken, shy and bright,
Glistening gems in velvet night.
Silhouettes in dance, they glide,
Secrets of the dusk abide.

Moonbeams shimmer on the lake,
Rippling softly, hearts awake.
Mysterious paths call us near,
Veils of twilight, crystal clear.

Wings of Transformation

A caterpillar dreams of flight,
In shadows deep, it yearns for light.
Cocooned in silence, time a friend,
Metamorphosis, the soul's ascend.

Colors burst in radiant bloom,
From stillness rises magic's plume.
Wings unfurl to greet the day,
Freedom's song will pave the way.

From earth to sky, a wondrous shift,
In every heart, there lies a gift.
Embrace the change, let spirits soar,
Life's a canvas, forevermore.

Beneath the Azure Horizon

Where oceans kiss the radiant sun,
Dreams awaken, journeys begun.
Waves like whispers, secrets shared,
Beneath the sky, we're unprepared.

Footprints dance on golden sand,
Stories crafted by fate's hand.
Horizons stretch, horizon wide,
Adventures beckon, hearts collide.

Seagulls cry in playful cheer,
Nature's voice, melodious clear.
Together under azure skies,
Where wonder blooms and spirit flies.

A Dance of Celestial Tides

The moon descends in silver flow,
Guiding waves through ebb and glow.
Stars reflect in ocean's sigh,
A dance of tides beneath the sky.

Harmony in cosmic dance,
Planets swirl in timeless trance.
Galaxies in twirling grace,
Invite the heart to find its place.

In every splash, a story told,
Of dreams and wishes bright and bold.
As the cosmos twirls its threads,
The dance of tides, forever spreads.

Fire on the Waters

Flames dance upon the waves,
Whispering secrets on the breeze.
Eagles soar in the twilight,
Chasing shadows with such ease.

Mirrored in the depths below,
Stars ignite the night's deep hue.
A canvas of dreams and hope,
Wrapped in a fiery view.

Each flicker tells a tale,
Of lovers lost and found anew.
While water sings its song of old,
In a world both bright and blue.

The horizon blurs with colors,
As darkness meets the light's embrace.
At the edge of every heartbeat,
Fire and water share a space.

In the end, the spirits dance,
With joy that sparkles like the sun.
For fire on the waters glows,
A fleeting moment, never done.

The Tides of Transcendence

The ocean breathes in whispers,
Drawing all thoughts to its core.
With every wave that rises,
You feel your spirit soar.

In the rhythm of the waters,
Time flows like a silver thread.
Each pulse a promise echoing,
Where dreams and memories are fed.

Boundless horizons beckon,
Where the sky and sea unite.
Caught in the tide's own rhythm,
You drift towards the light.

Old mariners' songs resound,
Their wisdom lost in the foam.
Each note a salty breeze,
Leading the heart back home.

Within the tides of transcendence,
You find your purpose, your place.
For the ocean holds all wonders,
In its vast and warm embrace.

Beneath the Celestial Canopy

Underneath the starlit quilt,
A tapestry of dreams takes flight.
Whispers of the night gently call,
Offering solace in their light.

The moon a guardian above,
Casting shadows on the waves.
While the cosmos sings its lullaby,
In the hearts of those it saves.

Beneath this celestial canopy,
Time stands still, yet flows like sand.
A symphony of love and hope,
Reaches out with a gentle hand.

Clouds drift like thoughts unspoken,
Each one a story lost at sea.
And as the night wraps round us,
We find our own tranquility.

In the glow of distant stars,
We dance with shadows of the past.
For beneath the celestial canopy,
Our dreams forever will last.

Dusk's Embrace in Aquatic Hues

As the sun slips into the sea,
The world is painted in gold and blue.
Dusk's embrace wraps around us,
In whispers soft and true.

The colors shift like gentle tides,
With each brushstroke, a new delight.
Reflections dance on water's skin,
As day concedes to night.

In this moment of perfect calm,
Nature's beauty takes its stance.
With every shade, a subtle charm,
In which our spirits prance.

The horizon bleeds with crimson dreams,
As stars begin to peek and play.
A soft serenade lingers on,
As twilight steals the day.

In dusk's embrace of aquatic hues,
We find ourselves, lost and found.
For every heartbeat shares a tale,
In the quiet, sacred sound.

The Alchemy of Aquamarine Dreams

In depths where whispers softly glow,
Aquamarine secrets ebb and flow.
Waves of wonder, a gentle tide,
Where dreams and starlight coincide.

A potion brewed in twilight's grace,
With shimmering glints, a radiant trace.
Infinity dances in the blue,
Awakening heartbeats, pure and true.

Mirrored skies reflect the soul,
In tranquil realms, we become whole.
With every drop, we dare to dream,
In places where the magic seems.

A net of clouds, a bridge of light,
Casting spells throughout the night.
In silence, mysteries unfold,
An alchemist's touch, a heart of gold.

With every wave that kisses sand,
We touch the void; the dreams expand.
Through aquamarine roads we roam,
Finding in the depths our home.

Celestial Waters Beneath the Stars

Beneath the stars, the waters gleam,
A night of wonders, a wistful dream.
Flickers tattoo the velvet skies,
While sleepy waves sing lullabies.

The heavens cradle secrets old,
Reflecting tales in silver and gold.
Every ripple a story unfolds,
In celestial whispers, the night beholds.

Galaxies dance in the moon's embrace,
As time drifts past in a gentle chase.
In stillness, the universe breathes deep,
While cosmic waters peacefully sleep.

Stars like lanterns float above,
Each twinkling spark, a promise of love.
In their glow, we cast our fears,
While patience flows like quiet tears.

So dip your toes in dreams untold,
In celestial waters, brave and bold.
Look to the heavens; allow them to steer,
This magical realm will draw you near.

The Phoenix's Crystal Waters

In fiery realms where legends soar,
A phoenix stirs from ancient lore.
Amongst the flames, a crystal stream,
Reflects the twilight's brilliant gleam.

From ashes born, pure flames ignite,
In waters bright, the dawn takes flight.
Each droplet holds a tale of old,
Of grace and strength, of hearts consoled.

The phoenix flutters, wings ablaze,
A dance of shadows in the haze.
While crystal waters weave their spell,
In every ripple, a story to tell.

Amidst the glow of dreams reborn,
A journey new in skies of morn.
In shimmering depths, all fears dissolve,
As sacred waters help us evolve.

With every splash, the past ignites,
New crescendos on wondrous nights.
The phoenix whispers, hopes anew,
In crystal waters, dreams come true.

Dreams in Shades of Blue

A twilight hush wraps night in blue,
While echoes of dreams come softly through.
Shades of azure brush the skies,
Whispering secrets in gentle sighs.

Waves of cobalt cradle the shore,
Where wishes linger, forevermore.
Each drop a promise, a flicker of light,
In the heart of shadows, dreams take flight.

The sea breathes life in tones so deep,
As moonlit dances stir from sleep.
In a canvas vast, our hopes align,
Painting futures in colors divine.

Beneath this azure, our spirits soar,
Unfurling wings as dreams explore.
In depths of night, the soul finds peace,
In shades of blue, all worries cease.

So dive into the ocean's embrace,
Where every wave is a sacred lace.
In the hues of night, forever stay,
Where dreams in shades of blue will play.

The Dance of the Radiant Navigator

In the realm of starlit skies,
A navigator with glowing eyes,
Guiding ships through night's embrace,
With every twinkle, a gentle trace.

Whispers of the sea, so clear,
Heralding dreams that draw us near,
As waves unite in rhythmic sway,
The dancer twirls, come what may.

Across the abyss, she weaves her song,
A symphony where night belongs,
With every movement, a story spun,
In the heart of the mariner's fun.

The moonlight kisses each wooden bow,
As silver trails mark the journey now,
Guided by stars, she leads the fleet,
In harmony, their destinies meet.

With laughter bright and spirits high,
The radiant navigator bids goodbye,
To a world where light forever gleams,
In the dance adorned with sailor's dreams.

Luminescence at the Water's Edge

By the banks where waters play,
Soft light flickers at the end of day,
Reflections dance on the gentle tide,
Inviting whispers to take a ride.

The moon spills silver on rippling dreams,
While quiet creatures share their schemes,
Each shadow skims the velvet shore,
As stars awaken to explore.

Inspiring tales the lanterns weave,
Of ancient times that we believe,
And echoes calling from the deep,
To waken souls and secrets keep.

The lapping waves, a soothing sound,
Where magic and reality abound,
As luminescence leads the way,
To secrets held till break of day.

At water's edge, our hearts take flight,
Embracing wonders hidden from sight,
With every glance, a spark ignites,
Beneath the glow of starry nights.

Melodies of a Shimmering Horizon

In the dawn's embrace, a treasure wakes,
With whispers soft from gentle lakes,
A melody borne on the shifting breeze,
As horizons shimmer and hearts find ease.

Each note ascends, a tale to tell,
Of lands beyond where dreams dwell,
Where sun meets sky in a swirling dance,
Inviting all to dare, to chance.

The colors splash in bold delight,
As daybreak banishes the night,
Creating harmony, bright and true,
With every dawn, the world anew.

From mountains high to valleys low,
The melodies flow, a river's flow,
Uniting hearts in joyous cheer,
As shimmering horizons draw us near.

In every whisper, a promise lies,
To soar above the endless skies,
With music sweet that time imparts,
Echoing softly in all our hearts.

Ascendancy of the Deep Waters

Beneath the waves, where silence reigns,
A kingdom thrives, free from chains,
The currents glide with stories old,
In depths where mysteries unfold.

Echoes of whales, a haunting song,
Flow through the realm where they belong,
As shadows dance in liquid grace,
The ocean holds an ancient face.

Fathoms deep, where colors gleam,
A vivid world, a dreamer's dream,
With coral castles and creatures rare,
An allure that draws us to repair.

In whispered currents, secrets thrall,
As tides embrace and rise and fall,
The deep waters beckon, soft and sweet,
Holding treasures beneath our feet.

And when the sun dips low each day,
The waves reflect its golden ray,
In the ascendancy of the deep,
Lies the beauty, where spirits seep.

A Dream Weaved in Shimmering Threads

In twilight's embrace, whispers hum,
As stars in the night begin to strum.
A tapestry spins with every glance,
Crafting a world where dreams advance.

Threads of silver dance through the air,
Weaving enchanted tales with flare.
From silken fibers, visions ignite,
A kaleidoscope born from purest light.

Each stitch a promise, each knot a vow,
In realms where hearts freely allow.
The fabric of hope in colors bright,
Awakens the spirit, igniting the night.

With every pull, the shadows flee,
Revealing what is yet to be.
In the loom of fate, we find our place,
As destiny weaves in sacred grace.

So close your eyes and breathe it in,
Allow the magic to begin.
For in this dreamscape, we shall find,
The shimmering threads that tie mankind.

Glimmers of Change in Starlit Waters

In waters deep, where secrets flow,
The starlit night begins to glow.
Glimmers rise as ripples play,
A dance of light at close of day.

Beneath the surface, futures gleam,
Each wave a whisper, a fleeting dream.
The moon reflects what lies ahead,
In tranquil light, our cares are shed.

Change softly nudges, like a breeze,
Bringing forth hope with perfect ease.
Out on the brink of something new,
We cast our wishes, bright and true.

As tides shift gently, time stands still,
Awakening hearts with every thrill.
A symphony of whispers sings,
Of unseen paths and wondrous things.

So let us sail on starlit seas,
With faith like sails, carried by ease.
For in this realm of dreams unfurled,
We find our place within the world.

The Enchantment of Midnight Reflections

The clock strikes twelve, the world holds breath,
In twilight's grasp, we conquer death.
Reflections shimmer on the lake,
Unveiling secrets that dreams can wake.

Silvered waters, like liquid glass,
Reveal the stories of those who pass.
With every ripple, a tale is spun,
Of quests embarked and battles won.

Midnight whispers secrets old,
Of wishes cast and dreams retold.
In every glance, a chance to see,
The hidden truths that set us free.

For in the dark, where shadows play,
The heart learns more than words can say.
Enchanted by the whispering night,
We grasp the stars, embrace the light.

So linger here, where echoes dwell,
In the midnight's magic, all is well.
For in reflections, we find our fate,
In dreams and hope, we illuminate.

Threads of Color in a Celestial Loom

In the heavens high, a loom extends,
Crafting colors through unseen bends.
Threads of twilight, of dawn's embrace,
Weave tales of wonder, of time and space.

Each hue a story, each tone a dream,
Spun from stardust in silver streams.
The cosmos sings in vibrant song,
Binding the threads where hearts belong.

Warm oranges dance with cooler blues,
Bright violets blend with vivid hues.
Under the gaze of a watching sky,
The canvas of life continues to fly.

As we reach out, our fingers trace,
The patterns of time, a soft embrace.
In this celestial tapestry so wide,
Our hopes and dreams forever abide.

So let us color with playful cheer,
Embrace the magic that draws us near.
For in this weave, we find our part,
Threads of connection, the beat of the heart.

Beneath the Mystical Shadow

In the grove where whispers dwell,
The old tree casts a timeless spell.
Beneath its boughs, the secrets flow,
Of dreams and fears we dare not show.

A flicker bright, a fleeting glance,
Under moonlight, fate finds its chance.
Shadows dancing, tales unwind,
In the heart, the truth we find.

Stars above in velvet night,
Guide the lost with gentle light.
Within the silence, echoes call,
Together we rise, together we fall.

Through the mist, a pathway gleams,
Leading us to forgotten dreams.
Every step, a choice to make,
Awake the world, awake the wake.

And when the dawn begins to break,
We'll cherish all that we forsake.
For beneath that mystical shadow,
Lies the heart of every meadow.

Reflections of a Rising Dream

In the crystal's gleaming light,
A world awakens from the night.
Waves of thought and purest grace,
Dance upon a silvered face.

Like a whisper caught in time,
Rising softly, sweet as rhyme.
Each reflection, a story bold,
Of wonders past and dreams retold.

Hope ignites, a blaze so bright,
Guided by the morning's light.
Burdened hearts find peace in flight,
As shadows fade away from sight.

And with each rise, a chance anew,
To weave together all that's true.
In the mirror of the sky,
The dreams awaken, soar and fly.

From the ashes of the night,
Heroes find their inner light.
Reflections speak in silent beams,
Leading us to waking dreams.

The Aquatic Firebird's Ascent

In the depths where waters gleam,
A firebird stirs from sacred dream.
With wings of flame, it cuts the tide,
In dance with currents, side by side.

Upwards it spirals, bright and bold,
A tale of courage yet untold.
The sea embraces, wild and free,
Life's wondrous journey, destiny.

Through coral gardens, colors blaze,
Awakening the mystic maze.
With every flap, the depths align,
Ancient stories intertwined.

It climbs the waves, a dazzling flight,
With heart ablaze, it seeks the light.
From ocean's cradle to the skies,
This firebird's spirit never dies.

Echoes of songs in ocean wells,
A tapestry of magic spells.
The aquatic firebird finds its place,
In every drop, its fiery grace.

Secrets Beneath the Velvet Sky

Beneath the stars, a canvas sprawls,
Whispers weave through moonlit halls.
A tapestry of dreams untold,
Wrapped in shadows, soft and cold.

The night reveals a hidden lore,
Of ancient paths, forevermore.
In every twinkle, stories dwell,
Of lost enchantments, cast a spell.

Silken breezes breathe the past,
In twilight realms, our hearts are cast.
Secrets linger, soft and sly,
Waiting for a curious eye.

So gather close, and hear the sound,
Of whispers that the stars surround.
In the velvet sky's embrace,
Find the magic, find your place.

For in the space where silence sings,
Lies the hope that midnight brings.
Secrets woven, profound and high,
Await the dreamers 'neath the sky.

The Color of Rebirth

In the garden, blooms awaken,
Petals soft, in dew they'll glisten.
Nature dons her fresh new robes,
Whispers promise, life encrobed.

Gentle winds begin to stir,
Paint the scene, in every blur.
Colors bright, a vivid dance,
Inviting all to take a chance.

Sapphire skies and emerald leaves,
Each chorus sings, and never grieves.
From winter's clutch, the earth breaks free,
A symphony of jubilee.

In every corner, shades ignite,
Painted dreams in morning light.
Hope emerges from every seed,
The color of rebirth indeed.

As shadows fade, the daylight yields,
To vibrant joys in sunlit fields.
Each heartbeat drives the new embrace,
In this realm, our souls find grace.

Flight Through Ether's Embrace

Upon a breeze, we dare to soar,
Where spirits dance and troubles pour.
Stars above in twilight's veil,
Guide the heart through unmarked trail.

A tapestry of endless night,
We chase the moon, in soft twilight.
Dreams unravel, weave through air,
In ether's hold, without a care.

Winds whisper secrets, softly spun,
Echoing tales of what's begun.
Through spectral realms, our visions trace,
In flight, we find our sacred space.

Let time dissolve, escape its clutch,
We touch the sky, feel heaven's hush.
In every heartbeat, magic flows,
Through ether's embrace, our spirit grows.

With wings unfurled, we chase the dawn,
On currents wild, we journey on.
In this adventure, free and bold,
The story of our souls unfolds.

Whispers of Hidden Depths

In the stillness, shadows weave,
Mysteries in whispers breathe.
Ancient echoes softly call,
Secrets wrapped in twilight's thrall.

Beneath the brook, where ripples play,
Silent wonders drift away.
Trees stand tall, their stories told,
In every ring, a heart of gold.

The moonbeams cast a silver spell,
Beneath the surface, deep we dwell.
With eyes closed tight, we sense the lore,
Of hidden depths, forevermore.

From every sigh the world intends,
Life's quiet song, it never ends.
In the silence, magic stirs,
In whispered truths, our spirit purrs.

To unearth treasures, they reside,
In the shadowed worlds we confide.
In every heart, a longing crests,
To find the whispers of the depths.

Between Dawn and Dusk

When shadows stretch and colors blend,
The day resigns, the night ascends.
Suspended time, a fleeting glance,
In twilight's glow, the world does dance.

Golden rays meet somber hues,
In silence grows the day's adieu.
A canvas vast where dreams take flight,
Between the day and coming night.

Stars awaken, one by one,
A tapestry of night begun.
Yet echoes of the day remain,
As softest sighs, a sweet refrain.

From dusk to dawn, a sacred space,
Where moments pause, and thoughts embrace.
In twilight hours, we find our peace,
Between the rhythms, life's release.

Here in the stillness, hearts align,
With every breath, the world will shine.
In quietude, our spirits trust,
The magic held between dusk and dawn.

Rising Flames in Sapphire Waters

In the depths where shadows flee,
Sapphire waters shimmer free.
Flames arise with vivid grace,
Dancing waves in warm embrace.

Whispers echo on the tide,
Where the secrets long abide.
Each spark ignites a tale anew,
Fragile dreams that dare break through.

With each flicker, colors blend,
Tales of hope that never end.
The night reveals a gilded way,
Where wishes weave and softly sway.

So let the flames and waters twine,
In this place where souls align.
For in the heart of sapphire blue,
Rising flames bring life to view.

Song of the Tamarisk Breeze

In a grove where whispers dwell,
Tamarisk sings a secret spell.
Softly swaying, branches sway,
Carrying the night away.

Notes of freedom fill the air,
Gentle breezes, free from care.
Rustling leaves, a soft embrace,
Nature's song in this sacred space.

As stars twinkle with ancient lore,
The silk of night begins to pour.
Each breath taken, pure and light,
Guides the heart through velvet night.

Beyond the hills, where dreams are found,
In this hush, we're spellbound.
Hear the song of nature's weave,
In the breeze, it bids us believe.

The Journey of a Wandering Star

Across the sky, a lone star glides,
In its glow, a mystery hides.
Wandering through the vast expanse,
Calling forth the night's romance.

With each pulse, the cosmos sings,
A melody of timeless things.
Guided by the dreams we share,
A journey forged in hopes laid bare.

Through the darkness, sparkling bright,
Finding paths with whispers light.
Every twinkle, stories told,
Of adventures great and bold.

So chase the star, and cast your gaze,
Embrace the magic of its ways.
For in the wandering, we are free,
Lost and found in eternity.

Cobalt Waves of Rejuvenation

Cobalt waves crash with a roar,
Kissing shores forevermore.
Each surge brings a burst of life,
Quelling thoughts of worldly strife.

In the foam, a promise gleams,
Carried softly in our dreams.
With every tide, a chance to start,
Healing whispers from the heart.

Salt and spray, a cleansing air,
Washing worries without care.
Breathing deep, we feel the change,
A world renewed, no longer strange.

Let the waters guide our way,
Through the night and into day.
In cobalt hues, we find our voice,
In the waves, we learn to rejoice.

The Blue Symphony of the Celestial Rite

Beneath the moon's soft silver glow,
The stars in whispers start to show.
A melody of dreams takes flight,
In the blue symphony of the night.

The waves compose a soothing tune,
While shadows dance beneath the moon.
Each note a flicker, pure and bright,
In this celestial, wondrous rite.

The sky unfurls its canvas wide,
As secrets of the cosmos bide.
Within each sparkling, gleaming sprite,
Lies the heart of the endless night.

A symphony of tides and stars,
In endless play, the night is ours.
With every breath, we feel the light,
In the blue symphony, take flight.

Together, hand in hand we'll weave,
The dreams that gently make us believe.
In stardust whispers, pure delight,
The magic lives in our shared rite.

Journey of the Watersong

Through forests dark, the waters flow,
With melodies that softly glow.
A journey starts where rivers wind,
In whispers of the streams we find.

Each note of water, clear and true,
A symphony of the skies so blue.
We dance where flowers sway and sing,
To the heartbeats of awakening.

As ripples race through sunlit air,
The whispers call, a gentle dare.
To join the chorus, brave and strong,
In the serenade of the watersong.

Embrace the trails of every stream,
Where shadows mingle, and willows dream.
With echoes saying we belong,
In the embrace of the watersong.

So let us tread where rivers bend,
In laughter's wake, around each friend.
With every sip, the world feels right,
In the soft magic of the light.

Awakening at the Azure Realm

In morning's hush, a world awakes,
Where azure skies the earth embraces.
With tender whispers on the breeze,
The realm unfolds with gentle ease.

Emerald fields adorned with dew,
Touching the heart, so fresh and new.
Every petal wakes to the sun,
In this dance, life has begun.

Inviting spirits, soaring high,
Beneath the vast and endless sky.
The azure realm, where dreams take flight,
In waking's arms, we witness light.

A canvas brushed with endless hues,
Awakening to life's sweet muse.
In harmony, we find our way,
To feel the dawn, to greet the day.

With each soft sigh, life breathes anew,
In the azure realm, hopes come true.
As day unfolds, a precious gift,
In the light of love, our spirits lift.

Ocean Fireflies in Celestial　Riviera

Underneath the twilight's glow,
Ocean fireflies start to flow.
They flicker softly on the wave,
In the celestial riviera's crave.

With every spark, a tale is spun,
A dance of dreams beneath the sun.
Like stars released from heaven's grip,
In ocean's depths, our hearts will skip.

As whispers ride the gentle tide,
With every pulse, the worlds collide.
In serenade, the night unfolds,
In stories hidden, yet untold.

Illuminate the waterside,
With magic born from deep inside.
These fireflies weave a glowing lace,
In this enchanting, sacred space.

Together lost in ocean's sway,
Let time dissolve, and dreams convey.
In every shimmer, pure delight,
Ocean fireflies, guide our flight.

Rebirth Amidst Churning Tides

Amidst the tempest's wild embrace,
A whisper stirs, a silent space.
From chaos blooms the softest light,
Rebirth awakens through the night.

Upon the waves, new dreams arise,
A canvas bright beneath the skies.
The ocean's rage, a fierce ballet,
Transforms the dark to brighter day.

In hidden depths, old spirits call,
Their echoes rise, the shadows fall.
Each crest and trough, a tale untold,
Of hearts once lost, now brave and bold.

So let the waters shape your soul,
Embrace the tide, become the whole.
For in the churn, we find our way,
And weave our hopes in salt and spray.

With every wave, a chance to grow,
To dance with fate, to feel, to flow.
From stormy seas, we gain our flight,
Rebirth, a glow in darkest night.

High Above the Crescent Waters

Beneath the moon's soft silver gleam,
The waters whisper, softly dream.
Reflecting tales of night and grace,
In every ripple, a hidden face.

The stars, like secrets, twinkle bright,
In harmony with fading light.
They guide us through the dusky blue,
A tapestry of old and new.

High above, a world unknown,
Floating thoughts like winds have blown.
A crescent bow in twilight's glow,
Where dreams awaken, currents flow.

In stillness held, the silence sings,
Of ancient lore and earthly things.
We sail our hopes on gentle tides,
With courage born, where truth resides.

For every heart that dares to soar,
Will find the shores of something more.
So lift your gaze, embrace the night,
For in that dark, we find our light.

Shadows of Celestials Emerge

In twilight's hush, shadows arise,
Celestials weave their secrets wise.
From starlit depths, their stories flow,
In whispered tones, the ancients glow.

They dance upon the velvet skies,
Casting dreams where wonder lies.
Each shimmer hints at what we seek,
In cosmic scripts, our hearts will speak.

Through silver beams, the past entwines,
Forgotten paths, in fate's designs.
The shadows carve a brighter fate,
As time unfolds, we contemplate.

In quiet nights, the truths will show,
That even in the dark we grow.
For every shadow hides a spark,
A light that glows, igniting the dark.

So let us trace the starry light,
And dance along the edge of night.
With every step, a new dawn waits,
As shadows yield to love's sweet fates.

A Chorus of Light and Depth

In harmony, the stars align,
A chorus sings of space divine.
Where light and depth in union blend,
And every note, a heart can mend.

The moonlight spills on tranquil seas,
In melodies that ride the breeze.
With every wave, a song is spun,
A symphony of moon and sun.

In every shadow, depth reveals,
The quiet strength that sorrow heals.
For in the darkness, light will bloom,
As hope descends to lift the gloom.

So join the dance, let voices rise,
In celebration of the skies.
Together, we can find our way,
Through night and day, come what may.

For in this world of ebb and flow,
A chorus sings, a vibrant glow.
With every heartbeat, let it start,
A symphony that binds our heart.

Harmony Between Fire and Flow

In a realm where embers gleam,
Rivers dance with silver dreams.
Fires crackle, whispers low,
Together, they create a glow.

Waves and flickers, side by side,
Nature's forces, wild and wide.
In the warmth, the waters play,
Holding secrets of the day.

Energetic spirals twine,
Heat and flow in grand design.
Every flicker, every wave,
A living tale that time won't cave.

The heart of nature, fierce and sweet,
In unity, they find their beat.
From the flames to liquid's grace,
Together, they embrace their place.

Harmony of opposites strong,
In this world, they both belong.
Fire and flow, a grand ballet,
A tapestry of night and day.

The Surreal Watercolor Skies

Brushstrokes of a painter's dream,
Whispers carried on the stream.
Clouds like pigments, soft and bright,
Blend beneath the waning light.

Crimson, azure, twilight's hue,
Sailing winds invite the view.
Sky to canvas, nature's hand,
Colors mingle, boldly stand.

In this realm where visions soar,
Myriad hues on heaven's floor.
Swirls of madness, calm embrace,
Nightfall's shadows find their place.

Textured thoughts of day's retreat,
Kaleidoscope of dreams complete.
Each hue a memory untold,
Stories beckon, brave and bold.

Surreal sunsets, twilight's sigh,
Infinite shades, no need to try.
A watercolor song, a lull,
In the silence, beauty's pull.

Cumulus Dust and Oceanair

Cumulus clouds in playful dance,
Whispers floating, lost in trance.
Dust of dreams from skies above,
Kissed by currents, pure as love.

The ocean's breath, a gentle sigh,
Meets the dust drifting by.
Tender waves wrapped in the blue,
Grasping memories, old and new.

Softly swaying, ebb and flow,
Nature's secrets, tides bestow.
Dappled shadows, sunlight beams,
Dreamers gather, lost in dreams.

Together they weave a tale,
In the air, where thoughts set sail.
Cumulus dust and ocean's grace,
In harmony, they find their place.

Every gust, an echo bright,
Filling hearts with pure delight.
Clouds and waves, a dance profound,
In their embrace, hope is found.

Where the Flame Meets the Current

In the shadows where they meet,
Flames ignite, waters greet.
A collision of fierce and free,
An elemental symphony.

Rippling surfaces reflect the fire,
Kindling hearts, igniting desire.
Murmurs coax the sparkle bright,
In stillness, chaos takes its flight.

Together they forge a new path,
Creating warmth amidst the wrath.
Tidal waves and crackling air,
In quiet moments, magic rare.

Verses of nature, fierce embrace,
Flame and current, time and space.
Where one ends, the other begins,
In their union, life ascends.

A dance of energies unfold,
In every flicker, truth is told.
Where the flame meets the current's song,
In their arms, we all belong.

The Dance of Light and Wave

In the shimmer of dawn, the waters gleam,
Waves whisper secrets, weaving a dream.
Lights twirl and twist, in vibrant embrace,
Nature's grand ballet, a moment's grace.

Beneath the sun's glow, a soft energetic race,
Ripples of laughter, a serenade's trace.
The wind joins the fun, a playful refrain,
Each crest and each trough, a ballet of gain.

Colors collide, in radiant delight,
Marrying shadows with strokes of bright.
The earth holds its breath, in awe of the show,
As light dances freely, in ebb and in flow.

No chains can contain this waltz of the free,
A moment expanding, vast as the sea.
And when twilight falls, the stars take their turn,
To mimic the waves, as the heavens yearn.

Thus flows life's great rhythm, in constant array,
The dance of light, oh, forever shall play.
With heartbeat of ocean, and whispers of air,
A symphony woven beyond all compare.

A Journey Through Celestial Currents

From stardust we rise, through galaxies wide,
On currents of dreaming, together we glide.
Every pulse of the stars, a beacon to find,
The tales of the cosmos, entwined with our mind.

With comets as arrows, we soar through the night,
Veering paths etched in the glow of starlight.
Through nebulae swirls, in colors so rare,
We glimpse at the wonders, rejoicing with flair.

Galaxies spin, in a symphonic reel,
Curving through time, as if part of a wheel.
Each moment's a treasure, each whisper a sign,
The essence of magic, in this grand design.

We ride on the winds of celestial lore,
Among the vast realms, forever explore.
In spirals and trails, our spirits unite,
A journey unfolding, bathed in soft light.

As dawn approaches, with a gentle embrace,
We carry the universe, boundless in space.
In the heart of the journey, each star will ignite,
Our dreams will dance freely, in pure cosmic light.

When Azure Meets Ember

In the cradle of twilight, where blue kisses red,
Azure meets ember, where dreams dare to tread.
The horizon alights, with whispers of fire,
As day softly bows to the night's sweet desire.

Stars shimmer like embers, in velvet so deep,
While silence envelops, as shadows creep.
Each color collides, a canvas anew,
A masterpiece painted, in shades of the hue.

The sky wears a gown, of both calm and of rage,
A story unfolding, from page onto page.
In the merge of the worlds, the heart finds its home,
In the clash of the colors, no more need to roam.

With the pulse of the evening, a melody sighs,
As dusk sweeps the air, with soft lullabies.
When azure meets ember, a magic is spun,
In the dance of the heavens, two souls become one.

And when night takes over, a cover so bold,
The secrets of twilight, in whispers unfold.
A tapestry woven, with emotion so bright,
Where azure meets ember, love conquers the night.

Radiance in the Depths of Flight

In a realm above, where the wild winds weave,
The heart finds its rhythm, begins to believe.
With feathers of hope, we take to the sky,
In radiant splendor, we learn how to fly.

The clouds, like pillows, soften our race,
While sunlight ignites every delicate space.
In the depths of our flight, we uncover our soul,
Where moments are fleeting, yet endlessly whole.

As we soar through the azure, so vast and so grand,
We paint with pure freedom, with dreams in our hand.
Each gust carries whispers of stories untold,
In the dance of the air, our spirits unfold.

With each rise and fall, our spirits take wing,
In the embrace of the clouds, we learn how to sing.
With grace we shall glide, through the luminous night,
In the depths of our journey, we find our own light.

So let the winds carry us far and so high,
With hearts intertwined, we will never say goodbye.
For there's radiance found, in each daring flight,
A brilliance that dances, in endless delight.

Twilight Currents in Celestial Waters

In twilight's embrace, the waters gleam,
Where whispers of starlight softly stream.
Currents of magic in twilight swirl,
As dreams on the surface gently unfurl.

Beneath the moon's gaze, secrets abide,
The dance of the tides, an ancient guide.
Voyagers drift through the shimmering night,
In celestial waters, hearts take flight.

Each ripple tells tales that time has spun,
Echoes of laughter, of battles won.
In the stillness, a promise resides,
As twilight currents with destiny glide.

A symphony sings in the depths below,
With every wave, a new story flows.
Reflections that shimmer, both near and far,
In twilight's embrace, we find who we are.

The Soaring Spirit and the Whispering Waves

On the breath of the sea, a spirit takes flight,
Carried by whispers, on winds of delight.
With wings like the sunlight, so golden and bright,
It dances through dreams in the hush of the night.

The waves sing a lullaby, soft and sweet,
As the spirit ascends, in rhythmic heartbeat.
Each crest and each trough, a magical sway,
Guiding the wanderer through twilight's ballet.

In the arms of the ocean, the soul finds its way,
Embracing the freedom of night and the day.
With laughter like currents, it rises anew,
In the symphony woven where skies meet the blue.

Soared high above, the spirit will roam,
Amidst the whispers, it finds its true home.
A journey unending, in waves full of grace,
Where the heart learns to dance in a boundless space.

Embracing the Hues of Twilight Flight

As dusk begins painting the sky with its brush,
The hues come alive, no need for a rush.
Every shade tells a story, rich and profound,
In the twilight's embrace, true magic is found.

Soft lavender whispers through shadows of night,
Invoking the dreams that take wing in their flight.
Against the deep indigo, stars softly gleam,
As twilight unveils the heart of a dream.

The brush strokes of twilight, a gentle caress,
Awakening feelings that so long were suppressed.
The dance of the colors, a moment's delight,
As the world wraps itself in the soft glow of night.

Through cerulean hues, courage takes form,
Embracing the twilight, a spirit reborn.
As the skies shift in shades of enchanting lore,
We find our own rhythm, forever to soar.

When the Sky Dances with Fire

When the sky dances, igniting the night,
With flames of the sunset, a glorious sight.
Crimson and gold swirl in one fervent heat,
As day bows to night in a radiant feat.

The horizon ignites, a magnificent blaze,
In awe, we stand struck by nature's grand ways.
Each flicker of light tells a tale of its own,
In the heart of the fire, new seeds are sown.

With passion and fervor, the stars start to wake,
As twilight unfolds, the earth starts to shake.
In the dance of the fire, we see our desires,
For within each spark lies the truth of our fliers.

Embers ascend to the velveted skies,
Carrying wishes where dreams start to rise.
When the sky dances fiercely, hearts come alive,
In the brilliance of flames, our spirits will thrive.

Mysteries Wrapped in Sapphire Veils

In twilight's grasp, secrets sleep,
Veils of sapphire, shadows creep.
Whispers dance on the cool night air,
Tales of old, hidden with care.

Beneath the moon's silvered glow,
Ancient paths that few will know.
Stars align, a cosmic guide,
Through the dark, where dreams abide.

In the forest, where fireflies play,
Cloaked in magic, they find their way.
Each flicker tells a story untold,
Of a world alive, of wonders bold.

With every rustling leaf and sigh,
Echoes of time, they softly fly.
Mysteries shrouded, yet so near,
Awakening hearts that dare to hear.

A spellbound journey, a whispered fate,
In this realm where shadows wait.
Sapphire veils, a shimmering seam,
Lost in the folds of a waking dream.

The Firefly's Journey through the Night

A flicker bright amidst the gloom,
The firefly dances, dispels the doom.
With every flash, a flick of fate,
Guiding the lost, never late.

In gardens dense, where silence reigns,
It weaves through shadows, light retains.
A tiny lantern, a tender spark,
Illuminating paths within the dark.

Across the fields, where whispers drift,
It flutters soft, a glowing gift.
Through the night, its journey flows,
Tracing the dreams that silence sows.

In secret nooks, where wishes lie,
The firefly glows, a watchful eye.
A waltz of radiance, pure delight,
Through endless hours, into the night.

Ode to the brave in the twilight's kiss,
A guide that carries hope and bliss.
For in its light, the world takes flight,
The firefly's journey through the night.

The Phoenix's Sojourn in Marine Depths

In whispered depths where shadows dance,
A phoenix stirs, a sea-glow glance.
Its fiery heart, a treasure fair,
Riding the waves, beyond despair.

Through coral groves, where silence sings,
It dives deep down on ocean wings.
With every pulse of the azure tide,
A saga blooms, in dreams it rides.

Caught in the currents, lost yet found,
The phoenix whirls in a vibrant round.
With scales of flame, it lights the deep,
Awakening secrets in slumbering sleep.

From depths it rises, aflame with grace,
Emerging bright in another place.
A dance of rebirth, fierce and bold,
In waves of wonder, its tale is told.

So let it soar, where the waters play,
A beacon bright, to guide the way.
In marine depths, its spirit weaves,
The phoenix's sojourn, in ocean leaves.

Dreams of an Elysian Tide

Upon the shore where dreams reside,
The waves unfold a tranquil tide.
In golden hues, the sunsets blend,
A fading day, where moments mend.

Each grain of sand, a story old,
Whispers of wishes, softly told.
With every crash, the sea's embrace,
Elysian realms, a sacred space.

Driftwood draped in sea's sweet song,
Fables linger, where hearts belong.
A perfect breeze fills the night's sky,
As moonlit glimmers invite a sigh.

In twilight's hush, the world feels light,
Shimmering dreams take flight that night.
A cosmic dance where souls converge,
In tides of peace, we gently surge.

O' swirling mists of softest grace,
The dreams of an Elysian place.
Together we sail, lost yet found,
In the tide of dreams, love knows no bound.

The Awakening of Celestial Beings

In twilight's hush, the heavens sigh,
Stars unfurl, like wings to fly.
Echoes whisper in the night,
Celestial beings glowing bright.

With each flicker, tales unfold,
Of lands beyond, both brave and bold.
Ancient eyes, in silence spark,
Revealing secrets in the dark.

They dance upon the moonbeam's grace,
A cosmic waltz, a timeless space.
Fragmented dreams, they intertwine,
As hearts awaken, souls align.

The midnight sky, a canvas vast,
With hues of blue, our shadows cast.
In unity, the stars will sing,
A hymn of hope that night can bring.

In wonder's grasp, the night transforms,
Through mystic paths and winding norms.
Celestial beings ever near,
In every heartbeat, they appear.

Unveiling the Terrestrial Secrets

Beneath the roots where shadows dwell,
Ancient whispers weave their spell.
In hidden glades where spirits tread,
The tales of earth in silence spread.

Footsteps follow loamy trails,
In the breath of leaves, the truth unveils.
The rhythm of the earth's own song,
Guides the seekers, brave and strong.

Rippling streams and aged stones,
Guarding stories, lost in tones.
A dance of life in every brook,
Nature's wisdom in every nook.

Winds carry scents of past embraced,
The echoes of the life once faced.
Each gentle breeze, a memory's call,
To unveil the secrets held by all.

In twilight's wane, the truth does gleam,
The earthly realm a woven dream.
Unmask the beauty, heed the plea,
For in the soil, our roots run free.

Refuge of the Cosmic Aquanaut

In depths of azure, the dreams reside,
Where ocean's heart and starlight bide.
A cosmic traveler, bold and bright,
Glides through realms of endless night.

With every wave, a story swells,
A symphony where silence dwells.
Beneath the tides, the wonders flow,
In the depths, the secrets grow.

Galaxies swirl in the ocean's embrace,
Each ripple shows a distant place.
The aquanaut, serene, profound,
Dances where the stars are found.

In moonlit paths of gentle sway,
He hears the ocean softly play.
With scales of light, the cosmos hums,
A refuge where the dreamer comes.

From deep within, the stories rise,
Woven back under twilight skies.
Inspired whispers, lost in time,
The cosmic aquanaut's sweet rhyme.

Fireflies Dancing on the Still Waters

In dusk's embrace, the fireflies gleam,
Flickering lights, a gentle dream.
They waltz above the shimmering lake,
Whispers of night, in silence wake.

Each spark of gold, a tale retold,
In emerald grass, their secrets hold.
The night air sings, a lullaby,
As stars above weave through the sky.

They dip and twirl, with pure delight,
Casting shadows, painting night.
Within their glow, the world stands still,
As nature breathes, and hearts fulfill.

Still waters mirror their radiant play,
Reflecting magic in soft array.
For in this dance, all fears may cease,
A moment captured, a glimpse of peace.

So linger long as night ensues,
Embrace the fireflies' mystic hues.
A fleeting glimpse of joy and grace,
In nature's heart, we find our place.

A Voyage Amongst Celestial Shores

Through cerulean tides we sail,
With stars above our guiding trail.
Whispers of the moonlit breeze,
Carry tales of mystic seas.

On waves of silver, dreams take flight,
As constellations gleam at night.
Each crest a story, wild and bold,
Adventures waiting to be told.

The horizon beckons, wide and vast,
Where echoes of the past are cast.
An endless dance of dusk and dawn,
On celestial shores, we journey on.

With every splash, the magic stirs,
In harmony, the melody whirs.
Together, we embrace the sea,
Boundless, wild, and truly free.

As we navigate through cosmic waves,
Nature's secrets, our hearts it saves.
In this voyage, we find our place,
Amongst the stars, a timeless grace.

The Call of Marina's Dawn

Awake, the shore, beneath the light,
Marina's dawn, a wondrous sight.
The gold and azure blissfully blend,
As the oceans' whispers gently send.

The seabirds dance in morning's play,
Heralding the brightening day.
Each ripple sparkles, fresh and new,
Inviting wonders and dreams to pursue.

With every wave, a secret sigh,
The world awakens with a cry.
For every dawn, there's magic spun,
In Marina's realm, where all begun.

The tides, they weave a tale of old,
Of sailors brave and treasures bold.
But in the hush, a promise lingers,
Of morning's peace, its tender fingers.

So let us heed the call of morn,
With hopeful hearts, anew reborn.
And chase the light, where dreams are drawn,
In the embrace of Marina's dawn.

Realm of the Shifting Colors

In twilight's grasp, the colors sweep,
A canvas rich, where shadows creep.
With strokes of magic, the world transforms,
In this realm, where wonder warms.

Violet skies kiss the azure sea,
In a dance of light, wild and free.
Emerald waves rise and fall,
Painting dreams on nature's wall.

Each hue tells stories, old, anew,
Of whispered magic, and skies so blue.
Fleeting moments, like dreams, unfold,
In a kaleidoscope of colors bold.

As the sun dips low, the colors flare,
A world alive, beyond compare.
With each transition, a glimpse divine,
In this realm, where hearts entwine.

So let us wander, hand in hand,
Through shifting colors, a promised land.
In the echoes of twilight's glow,
We find the magic that we know.

Traces of Twilight in Waters Unfathomed

In waters deep, where twilight lies,
Secrets dwell beneath the skies.
Each ripple holds a whispered tale,
Of journeys sailed, through storm and gale.

Beneath the waves, soft shadows play,
In search of light, they'll find their way.
With starlit glimmers, they ignite,
The dreams of all, hidden from sight.

The twilight traces, a silken thread,
Weaving stories of the long since dead.
In fathoms deep, where echoes blend,
The whispers of the sea transcend.

So let the depths be your embrace,
A voyage into that sacred space.
In waters unfathomed, truths will shine,
With twilight's grace, so pure, divine.

With open hearts, we dive profound,
In mysteries of the sea unbound.
For in each wave, a song awaits,
In twilight's arms, our fate creates.

A Transformation in the Wings of Night

In shadows deep, the secrets hide,
A whisper soft, where dreams reside.
The moonlight weaves its silken thread,
Transforming night, where hopes are led.

A gentle breeze, a fleeting sigh,
Through branches low, the spirits fly.
In twilight's grasp, we find our light,
Awakening forms in the arms of night.

The stars align in cosmic dance,
Entwined in fate, a fated chance.
As darkness blooms, the magic sings,
And change arrives on shimmering wings.

With every heartbeat, worlds immerse,
In whispered tales of the universe.
From mysteries born of shadow's lore,
We rise anew, forevermore.

The Luminous Water's Edge

By shores of silver, light is found,
Where gentle waves caress the ground.
Reflecting dreams in crystal streams,
Here magic flows, and starlight gleams.

The calm embrace of nature's grace,
Awakens joy in this serene space.
With every ripple, stories unfold,
Of secrets hidden, yet to be told.

In twilight's hue, the waters sway,
As dusk breaks forth into the day.
With echoing songs from depths below,
The heart of life begins to glow.

A dance of shadows, bright and dark,
Each splash ignites a vibrant spark.
At water's edge, we stand in awe,
Embracing wonders that nature drew.

Flight of the Celestial Fire

Above the clouds, the fiercest blaze,
A comet's tail through night's embrace.
With flaming wings, it carves the sky,
In search of dreams that dare to fly.

Each flicker holds a tale untold,
Of cosmic journeys, brave and bold.
Through limitless realms, it roams so free,
A radiant spark, eternally.

As galaxies swirl in endless dance,
The universe holds its breath in trance.
With every heartbeat, the wonders soar,
Celestial fire, forevermore.

Beneath, the world gazes at the night,
Awe-inspired by that fleeting light.
For every life with its own desire,
Finds hope in the flight of celestial fire.

The Paradox of Heat and Depth

In shallow pools where warmth resides,
The surface hides the depths inside.
A paradox wrapped in a gentle plea,
Where heat and depth weave mystery.

Beneath the sun, the waters gleam,
Yet hidden truths drift in the dream.
As layers fold, the layers burn,
In depths below, we long to learn.

With every ripple, we collide,
A dance of warmth that won't subside.
In every depth, a spark remains,
To tease the heart, to heal the pains.

A journey wrought by nature's might,
Through shadows cast by radiant light.
To seek the soul in what we find,
In paradox, we're intertwined.

The Swell of Possibilities

In the hush of dawn's embrace,
Whispers dance on the morning breeze,
Each breath carries a spark of grace,
Dreams unfold like a gentle tease.

Rippling waves of untold fate,
Cradle hopes beneath the sky,
With every beat, new realms await,
As stars wink softly, drifting by.

Paths untraveled lie ahead,
Moments flicker like fireflies,
Through shadows, light and laughter spread,
Awakening our hidden sighs.

With hearts alight, we dare to dive,
Into the swell of what could be,
In each pulse, we come alive,
Embracing all we cannot see.

So let the tide of wishes flow,
For in this vastness, magic sings,
In the currents, hope will show,
The beauty that tomorrow brings.

Phoenix Dreams in Ethereal Waves

Beneath the moon's enchanting glow,
A phoenix stirs with wings afire,
In dreams that shimmer, soft and slow,
Dance through the night, rising higher.

Each feather dipped in twilight's hue,
Echoes of ancient tales unfold,
In ethereal realms, wild and true,
Where the heart's secrets become bold.

Sailing on waves of timeless lore,
Carried by winds of whispered past,
Awakening desires we adore,
In flames of courage, shadows cast.

With every surge, rebirth ignites,
As starlit songs embrace the night,
With every flicker, a journey writes,
A tapestry of hope and light.

So spread your wings, let visions soar,
Through otherworlds, boundless and free,
In phoenix dreams, forevermore,
Let your spirit find its decree.

Harmonies of Ash and Tide

On the shore where whispers blend,
Ashen memories dance with the sea,
Harmony found in the heart's mend,
Together in their timeless decree.

With each wave, stories intertwine,
Carved in grains of sand and stone,
In fragile notes of love divine,
Echos linger in twilight's tone.

From fiery embers, life unfolds,
While tides reclaim what once was lost,
In the depths, a beauty unfolds,
Navigating through dreams embossed.

With every crest, a whisper calls,
Inviting hearts to seek and yearn,
In the mingling of rise and falls,
Infinite lessons we discern.

As ash meets tide, we rise anew,
Crafting dawn from remnants of night,
In the dance of shadows, we pursue,
The harmonies of life's delight.

Celestial Wings on Liquid Canvas

In twilight's grace, the heavens spread,
A canvas wide, with colors bright,
Celestial wings where dreams are led,
In the sky's embrace, pure delight.

Each stroke, a wish upon the breeze,
Painted whispers in the air,
As stardust flows in gentle ease,
Merging realms beyond compare.

Through liquid spells, we dare to fly,
Gliding softly, hearts unchained,
With radiant hues, we touch the sky,
In this moment, joy is gained.

In flight we find our sacred space,
A tapestry of hopes unfurled,
With every dip and soaring grace,
We craft the dreams that shape our world.

So spread your wings, let spirits sing,
On canvas vast, let colors gleam,
In celestial dance, forever cling,
To the brilliance of a shared dream.

The Reverie of a Dying Flame

A flicker in the shadowed room,
A warmth that wrestles with the gloom.
Memories dance in amber light,
Whispers of a fading night.

The logs curl softly to their end,
Each crackle a tale, a once dear friend.
Time drips slowly, like a tear,
As dawn approaches, drawing near.

In dreams of fire, we find our peace,
In every ember, heart's release.
Though ash may claim what once was bright,
Hope lingers still in the soft twilight.

A final spark, a shimmered sigh,
When shadows stretch and embers die.
We bid adieu, let go the flame,
Yet in our hearts, it lives the same.

For every blaze that flickers low,
Is but a guide to futures' glow.
And in the hollow of this night,
We chase the dreams that take to flight.

Dreams on the Edge of Twilight

Amidst the twilight's gentle hues,
Soft whispers float in silken views.
Where dreams entwine with dusky skies,
And laughter melds with nightbird cries.

The world's aglow with softest grace,
As stars peek out to join the chase.
Guided by hope, we dare to roam,
On paths where shadows call us home.

In secret corners of the mind,
Where magic stirs and tales unwind.
We dance on edges, breathe the air,
Of dreams that glimmer everywhere.

So let the dusk enfold your fears,
And hold the moment, dry your tears.
For every end brings forth a start,
In twilight's glow, we find our heart.

With heavy eyes, we drift to sleep,
Embracing dreams, their secrets keep.
In slumber's realm, the wild takes flight,
As dreams unfold in the edge of night.

When Stars Merge with the Sea

Beneath the velvet sky, they gleam,
Stars dip down into the dream.
Where ocean waves, in rhythmic flow,
Embrace the light, soft ebb and glow.

Their twinkling whispers brush the tide,
And in the depths, their spirits glide.
Together, they weave a wondrous tale,
Of night's embrace on a silver trail.

When ripples dance and secrets sigh,
The universe unfolds its eye.
As stardust mingles with the brine,
A cosmic love, a bond divine.

The moon, a bridge from sky to sea,
Illuminates what's meant to be.
In tides that pull, in currents strong,
The heart knows well where it belongs.

So let the waves and stars collide,
In every pulse, our dreams abide.
For when they merge, the night is whole,
And echoes deep within the soul.

Rhapsody of the Ascending Waves

In the dance of tides, a chorus swells,
A symphony that weaves and dwells.
Each wave a note in ocean's song,
Carrying whispers, deep and strong.

The surf ignites the sandy shore,
With every rise, it calls for more.
A rhapsody of liquid grace,
That spills like laughter, fills the space.

Frothy crowns upon each crest,
Nature's rhythm, a sacred quest.
From beastly roars to gentle sighs,
Each wave a tale that never dies.

As seagulls glide and sunsets blend,
The ocean's song will never end.
It lifts us high, it grounds us low,
In this embrace, our spirits grow.

So let the waves serenade the night,
With melodies that take to flight.
For in the sea, we find our way,
In rhapsody of the rising spray.

The Phoenix Speaks in Ocean Currents

In whispers soft, the phoenix calls,
From depths of blue, where silence falls.
With every wave, a story spun,
Of battles fought and battles won.

Its feathers glint like stars above,
Crafted tales of loss and love.
In ocean's dance, the secrets rise,
To paint the skies with fiery sighs.

Oh, flames that flicker, bright and bold,
In currents deep, their truths unfold.
From ashes sweet, new life appears,
A melody that calms all fears.

Through salty winds, the echoes sing,
Of timeless hope and new beginnings.
With every crest, the art shines clear,
As whispers fade, the phoenix cheers.

So heed the song of waters deep,
Where fire and ocean secrets keep.
For in the heart of every wave,
The phoenix hides, eternally brave.

Mirrored Flames in Riveting Blues

Reflections dance on waters bright,
Flames entwined in a magic light.
In depths of blue, the fire glows,
With every breath, the beauty flows.

Mirrored dreams in swirling hues,
Whispering the forgotten clues.
Each flicker held within our gaze,
Capturing both the night and blaze.

The blues embrace the ardent reds,
In wild spirals where passion treads.
A tapestry, rich and bold,
Of stories shared, and secrets told.

In twilight's hold, the colors blend,
Where time does stop, the heart can mend.
Through shimmering waves, the visions run,
In mirrored flames, all is one.

So let the rivulets guide your way,
Through mirrored flames, where spirits play.
For in each glow, a wonder gleams,
An endless dance of whispered dreams.

Wings Caught in Celestial Currents

Wings unfurl in the starry night,
Caught in currents, taking flight.
Beyond the clouds, they gently soar,
Through veils of light, forevermore.

With every gust, a tale unfolds,
Of cosmic paths and wonders bold.
In celestial realms, where wishes fly,
The wings embrace the boundless sky.

From stardust trails, they find their way,
In whispers soft, the night must sway.
A symphony of wings alight,
In dazzling dreams that chase the night.

Oh, how they twirl in endless grace,
Through airy heights, they find their place.
Each current sings, a lullaby,
That echoes through the cosmic high.

So let your heart, like wings, aspire,
To dance among the stars and fire.
For in the currents, bold and bright,
Your spirit soars, a wondrous sight.

A Serenade of Shifting Skies

Above the world, the colors shift,
A serenade, the heavens gift.
In hues of gold and twilight blue,
The sky unveils its canvas true.

With every brush, a story spun,
Of days departed and those to come.
A waltz of clouds, in graceful sweep,
Where stars await and shadows creep.

In dancing light, the moments freeze,
Each fallen star, a whispered breeze.
Through shifting skies, the visions play,
Echoes of night, the birth of day.

Awake the dreams within your soul,
As skies transform, and moments roll.
For in this dance, we find our way,
A serenade that will not sway.

So lift your gaze to heavens wide,
Where endless wonders will abide.
In every shade, a story flies,
A serenade of shifting skies.

Flights of Color in Starlit Waters

Beneath the stars where shadows play,
The waters glimmer, night turns to day.
Waves whisper secrets, soft and low,
As colors dance in a silvery flow.

In fuchsia, azure, and golden hue,
Fish leap like wishes, bright and true.
They spin through moonbeams with joyful grace,
A masterpiece painted on time's embrace.

The air is laced with magic's thread,
Dreams of the moon above our heads.
Each cresting wave, a lullaby sung,
In this watery realm, forever young.

Ripples shimmer with stories untold,
In this enchanted world, quietly bold.
Nature's brush, a master of fate,
Creates a wonder we soon await.

So let us sail on this dreamlike tide,
With hearts united, and eyes open wide.
For in starlit waters, we find our way,
In flights of color, together we stay.

The Elysian Echo of Changing Tides

Whispers of the ocean, soft and profound,
Call to the heart, in melody found.
Each wave a story, each ebb a song,
In the rhythm of tides, we all belong.

The sun dips low, painting skies aglow,
As dreams reshape like the flowing flow.
In colors of twilight, we learn to believe,
In the echoes of night, we learn to receive.

Clouds dance in laughter, silver and gray,
They journey with shadows, in majestic play.
Moments like whispers, so fleeting and bright,
Harness the magic—embrace the night.

Tides that are changing reflect our own plight,
With every new dawn, we chase the light.
In Elysian gardens where spirits align,
Every drop holds a memory, every wave a sign.

So sail with the currents, feel the embrace,
Of the ever-changing, timeless grace.
For in water's heart, we find our way,
In the echoing tides, we learn to stay.

A Fire's Embrace in the Deep Blue

A flicker of warmth amidst the deep,
Where shadows linger, and secrets keep.
In the heart of the ocean, flames dance bright,
A fire's embrace, a beacon of light.

The waves may howl, the winds may wail,
Yet here we stand, we will not fail.
With spirits ablaze, kindled by dreams,
We journey together, or so it seems.

As coral blooms in colors so rare,
In the depths of the abyss, we find our air.
Each blaze of fire beneath the sea,
Unfolds our stories, forever free.

So gather 'round this flickering flame,
In the realm of the ocean, forever the same.
For deep within, there lies a spark,
A fire's embrace, a dance in the dark.

Let us face the depths, hand in hand,
With courage that comes from the texture of sand.
In the ocean's heart, we find our place,
A fire's embrace, in a deep blue space.

Chasing Resplendence Beyond the Horizon

The horizon beckons with colors so bright,
A canvas of dreams woven by light.
With each step forward, our spirits ignite,
Chasing resplendence, chasing the night.

In lavender echoes of twilight's grace,
We wander through shadows, we frolic and race.
Stars twinkle like diamonds in the great above,
Guiding our hearts in a dance of love.

Every wave whispers of paths unexplored,
In the symphony of waters, we are adored.
Together we journey toward realms yet unknown,
In pursuit of the magic we can call our own.

Let the winds carry our hopes and our fears,
As we sail through the darkness, washed in our tears.
For in every sunrise, a promise unfolds,
Chasing resplendence, our story is told.

So rise with the sun, let our spirits unite,
In the journey ahead, through day and through night.
For the world is a tapestry, woven with dreams,
Chasing resplendence, beyond the moonbeams.

Blossoms of a Celestial Dream

In twilight's grace, the flowers bloom,
Whispers of hope in the night's soft room.
Their petals dance in the starlit air,
Dreams woven gently, a world laid bare.

Through azure skies where shadows weave,
The moonlight sings, and hearts believe.
Each fragrant breath, a secret shared,
In darkened gardens, the lost repaired.

With morning's light, the dreams take flight,
A symphony bright against the night.
Beneath the canopy of endless stars,
We find our way, despite the scars.

As blossoms twirl in cosmic streams,
They cradle long-forgotten dreams.
Under the guise of the velvet sky,
The echoes of wishes never die.

In delicate hues, the universe glows,
A promise held where the soft wind blows.
With each heartbeat, the magic sings,
A tapestry woven on ethereal wings.

A Tapestry of Stars and Waves

Upon the shore where oceans seethe,
Stars glance down, like dreams they breathe.
Their shimmering light on the water's crest,
An eternal dance, a timeless quest.

The waves caress the ancient sand,
A lullaby sung by nature's hand.
With every rise and every fall,
The cosmos answers a distant call.

Moonlit paths weave through the tide,
Where secrets dwell and dreams abide.
A tapestry spun with silver threads,
Connecting souls that fate embeds.

In the silence of night, the heart takes flight,
Guided by stars that burn so bright.
They whisper tales of journeys grand,
Of seekers lost in foreign lands.

In each wave, a story lies,
Of distant worlds and starlit skies.
Together they dance, forever entwined,
In the ocean's heart, true peace we find.

The Harmony of Celestial Currents

In the stillness where dreams collide,
Celestial currents in harmony glide.
Softly they whisper secrets untold,
In silver echoes, the brave and bold.

A river of stars through the night extends,
Each gleaming spark is a message it sends.
The universe hums a lullaby sweet,
Where stardust and whispers of magic meet.

In the breezes that swirl through eternity's halls,
Nature's own music around us calls.
A symphony played by the moon and the sun,
In timeless circles, the journey's begun.

With every heartbeat, the cosmos sways,
Guided by love on the celestial rays.
We dance in the light, lost in the flow,
While the currents of fate forever bestow.

From fragments of dreams, a tapestry weaves,
In the melody of night, the heart believes.
Together we rise, with the stars as our guide,
In harmony wrapped, we dare to abide.

A Pathway to Ethereal Shores

Through drifting clouds and misty skies,
A pathway opens where magic lies.
Each step we take on this tranquil path,
Leads us to realms that love bequeaths.

Voices of ancients whisper our name,
Guiding our hearts in a dance of flame.
With every heartbeat, lost dreams return,
Lighting the way as our spirits yearn.

With each soft wave that kisses the sand,
The echoes of time stretch hand in hand.
A journey unfolds to ethereal shores,
Where forever waits and wonder soars.

The sun dips low, painting skies aglow,
We stand in awe as the night winds blow.
Stars emerge, each a beacon bright,
Illuminating our dreams in flight.

On this pathway, we wander free,
Crafting a future, just you and me.
With hearts entwined as the shadows play,
We find our home where the skies turn gray.

Echoes of a Rising Sun

In the dawn's first light, a shimmer calls,
Whispers of hope dance on the walls.
Dreams take flight on golden beams,
Awakening hearts to their hidden dreams.

The world unfolds with each gentle rise,
Painting the skies in rosy dyes.
Nature's palette, vibrant and vast,
Holds the secrets of the past.

Birds soar high with a joyful song,
Guiding the lost who've wandered long.
As shadows flee from the sun's embrace,
Courage is born, and fears erase.

With every breath, the earth comes alive,
In this sacred moment, we thrive.
Echoes of laughter fill the air,
A promise of magic waits everywhere.

So rise with the sun, let your spirit roam,
In the warmth of the light, find your home.
For even the darkest nights must yield,
To the echoes of dawn, love's battlefield.

The Serpent's Breath in Lavender Skies

Beneath the whispers of twilight's grace,
A serpent coils in a mystical space.
Lurking gently with lustrous scales,
Breath like embers in enchanted trails.

Lavender hues stretch wide and far,
As secrets rise like a shooting star.
In the stillness, magic weaves,
A tapestry where no one leaves.

With eyes that glitter like ancient stones,
The serpent glides through twilight tones.
In shadows deep where the night does dwell,
Each breath a story, a whispered spell.

Dreamers wander in the dusky light,
Chasing echoes of the fading night.
For every breath that the serpent takes,
A new beginning in the stillness wakes.

In lavender skies, where mysteries flow,
The serpent teaches what dreams can sow.
To dance with shadows yet embrace the day,
In the twilight's grip, forever stay.

Ascension of the Mystic Fisher

By the river's edge, where tales are spun,
The mystic fisher casts for the sun.
With simpler nets woven from lace,
He beckons spirits in watery space.

The waters part with a silken sigh,
As echoes of dreams begin to fly.
In the shimmer, glimmers of fortune shine,
Promises held in each silver line.

With patience deep as the river's flow,
He waits for the whispers, the secrets to show.
Each ripple holds the universe near,
In stillness, he draws forth hope and fear.

Beneath the surface, the magic lifts,
As shadows take form in watery drifts.
Ascension calls to the chosen few,
To weave their fates with the morning dew.

When twilight falls, and the stars ignite,
The mystic fisher baits the night.
Casting dreams on a cosmic tide,
In the depths of hope, he shall abide.

Nocturne of the Emerald Depths

In the emerald depths where silence dwells,
A nocturne plays with hidden spells.
Ripples of green in moonlight glide,
Where secrets breathe and shadows hide.

A melody flows like the midnight breeze,
Enchanting the heart with whispered pleas.
Beneath the waves, a world awaits,
Inviting the timid through mystic gates.

Stars flicker down to brush the sea,
As the night unfolds its tapestry.
All creatures dance in their emerald homes,
As the water's lullaby gently roams.

With every note, the night unfolds,
Stories of dreams and legends untold.
In the depths of darkness, light does leap,
A noontime promise that night will keep.

So listen close to the ocean's breath,
In the emerald depths, embrace your quest.
For in the night where shadows blend,
The noontime song is never to end.